CHRISTIANS IN POLITICS

Unmuffling the Prophetic Voice

RICHARD LUCAS

BROWN
DOG
BOOKS

FOREWORD

"Does any other group enter the political fray holding that they ought not espouse their own values, or advocate measures reflecting them? I can't think of one. Christians seem unique in adopting this bizarre attitude of political self-elimination, while all-comers compete aggressively to mould policy and law in their own image."

The author exhorts political engagement at a time when the expression of Christian ideals in the public arena is becoming increasingly muffled. He takes on a string of fallacies that circulate among the faithful and induce "timidity, disengagement and deafening silence".

Instead of "meekly accepting the world's agenda", he urges, we must re-order our priorities and be confident of God's wisdom.

From the philosophical foundations to the nitty gritty of party politics, you will find this little book packed with original thought. The context is Scottish, but the principles are most definitely universal.

The incisive logic is compelling and challenging. It's a short book but it packs quite a punch.

This persuasive piece of writing just might mobilise Christians into political action and unmuffle our prophetic voice. Our nation needs it as never before!

Michael Willis
Chairman of the Scottish Family Party

PART 3: DEMOCRATIC INFLUENCE: USE IT OR LOSE IT!

HOW AND WHY SHOULD CHRISTIANS ENGAGE IN POLITICS?

Leading a political party leads to lots of conversations about politics, with all sorts of people, including Christians.

Most of the thoughts I share here have been generated by interaction with Christians of all hues and roles within the church. They are not so much about what Christians say about policy areas directly - that's usually fairly straightforward. The really interesting bit has been hearing the ideas about how, why and whether Christians should engage in politics. Many chapters in this book are inspired by a line I've heard from Christians in discussion.

This wide range of viewpoints has led me to reflect on Christian engagement in politics and distil my own thoughts. I present here a case for the positions I have arrived at.

The first part seeks to clarify our goal as Christians engaging in politics. What are we aiming to achieve? Why? Might we be distracted by other goals?

In the second part, I consider some of the factors that currently keep many Christians and Churches on mute in the political sphere. I seek to dismantle common fallacious arguments that serve to induce timidity, disengagement and deafening silence.

The third and final part tackles the nitty gritty of politics: elections, candidates, parties and governments. I question some views widely held in Christendom. Prepare to be challenged!

I will attempt to present my case through logic rather than through persuasive language, endeavouring to refrain from pejorative language about alternative views and positive rhetoric about my own. All that does is provoke the converse in response, leading to entrenched stalemate.

Biblical material will not be central to my arguments – not because it's not important, but because the issues I address are more about how to implement the vision laid out in Scripture. In my experience, many Christians are pretty clear on core moral teachings, but uncertainty and even confusion creep in at the practical application stage.

While the principles elucidated are illustrated in the Scottish context, the book is accessible and applicable to all.

There will be passages here that will challenge the central embodiment of Christian political mission in the lives of some. I don't take that lightly. The reader must accept my case or rebut it. I will be happy to read, discuss and respond to counter arguments.

From my own experience, I can affirm that when God has led me into something, that has not always meant that it was the ideal or final expression of a calling. There are lessons to learn along the way. While we may have felt God's guidance into our current form of political engagement, let's be open minded about our path in the future.

When I talk about Christian values or morals in politics, I am referring to areas where Christian teaching diverges from the mainstream consensus. So, for example, caring for the sick and providing for the poor are Christian imperatives but also part of the political consensus. Each party has its own approach to these activities and choosing between them is more a matter of practicality than of Christian principle. But when it comes to issues like assisted suicide, Christian principle is very much on one side of the political debate.

I know that many professing Christian faith contradict Biblical values as we understand them, so when I refer to "Christian principles" I mean the moral truths traditionally articulated by the mainstream Christian denominations.

"He would say that, wouldn't he?" might be your initial response to some of my points. I hope, however, that you'll be open to the possibility that my thinking has led me into my current role, rather than vice versa.

I'm always amused when I see introductory sections with headings such as "How to read this book." I expect advice such as "hold the book open, the right way up, in front of your face." But, undeterred, I'll offer some advice. The chapters are very short. I could have padded them out with quotations, analogies and illustrations galore, but I haven't, because the concepts are simple and do not require such buttressing. However, whether you read it in a single sitting on a beach deckchair or in short instalments in a small private room at home, I'd suggest you do one thing. After each section ask yourself the question, "Is he right?" Then "If not, why not?" or "If so, what does that imply for me?"

If this book can help you clarify your thoughts on political engagement as a Christian, mission accomplished! I hope that feedback and debate will help me further refine my thinking as well - do share your thoughts via richard.lucas@scottishfamily.org.

Ultimately, may God lead us in his wisdom.

PART 1
THE GOAL

THE FOUNDATIONS

Where shall we start?

Let's begin with some things all Christians will agree on, I hope!

1) God wants us to contribute to improving people's circumstances, reducing pain and suffering, maximising health, protecting from various dangers, and enabling fulfilling lives in a strong network of relationships. Agreed? Note I'm not saying that this is the sole or even primary aspect of God's will for us, but it is at least part of it.

2) One way that we can take part in this project is by presenting the central message of the Christian gospel, leading to some becoming Christians and joining the church. This has eternal significance beyond this world, but it also contributes to bringing about positive change here and now as lives are transformed.

   We can also contribute to the project by other means in addition to evangelism, many of which can be summarised in the instruction to love our neighbour.

   How's that sound? With me so far?

3) We take our mission to love our neighbour and create a better society into every aspect of our lives: personal and family relationships, church life, charitable work and giving. Our paid work almost certainly gives the opportunity to do good. Almost every job and career involves providing some benefit to society (unless you are a marketing manager for a cigarette company or such like). Every workplace also gives the opportunity to build positive and supportive relationships. We can also pursue this mission through political activity, at any level from voting to being

a politician. I know that a very small number of Christians believe that any form of political engagement is improper - I won't answer them here - but almost all of you will, in all probability, find yourself in agreement with my third point. It's hardly controversial.

4) God's Wisdom and moral standards are knowable through the Bible and/or the teaching of the church. These principles are good for people, leading to the sort of positive outcomes I referred to earlier, both for individuals and for a society. Examples of such Christian teaching are the institution of marriage, the absolute rejection of dishonesty and the exhortation to care for the sick. These are not arbitrary religious peculiarities, but vital principles on which to build a healthy society. Rejecting them will result in harm, individually and collectively. I expect you fully agree again - it's not a radical view. There might be some divergence of opinion about what these principles are exactly, but that doesn't undermine my point.

5) Politics should be about improving people's lot by bringing about and maintaining a society where all can flourish. Some may enter politics with less altruistic motives, but the mission to promote net wellbeing, freedom, justice and safety should be paramount. I'm not expecting an argument over this one either!

6) From point 5, it follows that each should bring their own understanding of how to create and maintain a healthy society into the political arena. From voters to the Prime Minister, the motivation should be to seek the good of society by supporting the policies sincerely believed to be most effective. Surely I'm just stating the obvious?

7) From point 4, it follows that, as Christians, at least part of our understanding of how to create and maintain a positive society for all will be informed by Christian principles. We have confidence in God's wisdom.

8) From points 3, 6 and 7, it follows that Christian principles should inform the political thinking and actions of all Christians, from voters to elected politicians.

These eight points constitute the starting point for engagement in politics by any Christian. Note that I haven't been addressing the role of the church or denominations - that's a question for later - but just individual Christians.

While Christians will bring a distinctive set of values, we should remember that no moral principle is unique to Christianity. Many of other faiths and philosophical persuasions also recognise the truth of Christian principles (though they might not agree that they are "Christian"). That's exactly what we should expect as God has given a conscience to all.

So, having laid the foundations, how do we build on them? That's what the rest of this book will be about.

Elucidating Christian principles is the easy bit: God's revelation and church tradition is clear on a very wide array of points. However, when it comes to implementing it practically, the path ahead seems more obscure. The Old Testament overflows with moral law, wisdom and social policy designed to form a great nation, but the context of Israel as God's chosen nation is radically different from our own. In the New Testament the moral teaching is clear, but little relates to influencing public policy.

So, when it comes to engaging in politics as Christians, we need to think it through for ourselves, following Biblical pointers and God's leading, but there will be much that we need to construct using our God-given reason.

But now we are clear where we start, at least: we hold a set of principles that are revealed by God which will help create a better society for all. Having been entrusted with this divine wisdom, our responsibility is to act on it for the good of our fellow human beings. And that includes through the political system.

I must avoid the error of exhorting all Christians to follow my calling into intensive political activity, but some degree of political engagement is surely required of each of us in a democratic nation? At least the decision-making process of who we vote for should be influenced by our Christian values.

Now that the foundation is laid, the sparks might start to fly as the building process commences!

REORDERING PRIORITIES

What fires you up? Which issues motivate you to take to the streets, or at least to fume at the TV? What drives you to political action?

Christians should not allow the mainstream of political and media debate to determine their own political priorities. For years, the news was full of Brexit, but that doesn't mean it was top of God's priorities. Christians, if their values are moulded by God, should find that their political passions are inflamed by some issues that mainstream parties neglect, and vice versa.

It can be hard to step back from the daily torrent of news, but our priorities should be ordered by Biblical teaching, not just the BBC. If we hold to orthodox Christian teaching, but our priorities are unaffected, we will not serve as salt or light. What a waste if Christians possess an understanding of divine wisdom, but never even mention a large portion of it because the news cycle never gives the cue.

Often Christians are called to be starting new debates rather than just pitching into whatever political controversy is raging at the time. We hand over too much power to the media and current political leaders if we allow them to set the agenda constantly.

A more serious problem still is that Christians can be caught up in the media/political maelstrom to the extent that they internalise the priorities of mainstream debate. As a result, they can believe that their own Christian convictions are somehow not to be regarded as valid or important in the political arena. Perhaps this is unsurprising as this message is often delivered, explicitly or implicitly, in forms such as, "Well that's just your personal religious belief, you shouldn't bring it into politics," or, "I really appreciate how you aren't one of those Christians who try to impose your views on people."

If we are to fulfil any prophetic calling, we need to be able to set the agenda, not just respond to other people's agenda. It can be an uphill struggle unearthing issues of the utmost moral gravity and publicising them while the news cycle is often filled with tribal mudslinging over relatively trivial and manufactured grievances. And this is compounded when Christians are as caught up in it as anyone. We need to be able to look beyond the headlines and assess what's really important.

In Scotland, it is assumed that the foundation of everyone's political outlook must be either nationalism or unionism. Not too long ago, remain/leave would have been considered equally basic. We must be careful not to infuse (or confuse!) our natural political inclinations with divine purpose. What should we be more concerned about, the constitution or the killing of thousands of unborn children every year in Scotland?

Party politics, from voting to joining a party, involves compromises. Which issues should be most pivotal in determining our allegiance? Should some immoral policies be deal breakers for Christians? We'll talk about this further in later chapters.

To conclude, if you are a Christian and your priorities are indistinguishable from the mainstream of political and media debate, I'd invite you to take some time to reassess. Yes, there is much common ground, but where God's standards are being inverted, it's our job to point to a better way - for the sake of the unborn, children, adults, families and wider society.

We can't allow ourselves to be crowded out of the debate by meekly accepting the world's agenda. We shouldn't keep the truth hidden away and out of the way. Didn't Jesus have something to say about that?

MAINSTREAM NARRATIVE ACCEPTERS AND DENIERS

"There are two sorts of people in this world…" So begins a host of simplistic folk "wisdom."

It's usually a simplified way of expressing an axis on which people vary: brave or timid, rash or reflective, calm or fiery, sociable or solitary - the list could go on indefinitely.

When it comes to political persuasion, axes usually include left/right, conservative/progressive, liberal/authoritarian and nationalist/globalist. But there is another one that I've noticed and it seems pretty foundational. It's this: mainstream narrative acceptor/denier.

Or, roughly speaking, from believing everything the BBC says to believing nothing that the BBC says. Or believing that everything that the government does is well-intentioned, to believing that it is all ill-intentioned. Quite a distinct dichotomy seems to have opened up, with a substantial majority in the first camp and a committed minority in the second.

Why has this polarisation emerged? I'm not at all sure, but I'll offer my theories.

Firstly, mainstream media such as the BBC have lost credibility in the eyes of many because they have evinced blatant bias and partiality. Once trust is damaged, it may well collapse completely.

Secondly, online alternative media now offer a counter-narrative on every issue under the sun, so scepticism towards every mainstream narrative can be buttressed by online commentators and experts, real or imagined.

Thirdly, as trust in politicians and political parties has decayed, the flames of extreme scepticism and cynicism have been fanned.

Fourthly, the burgeoning "alternative media" scene is comprised primarily of people seeking to make money out of it. There is no market for less professional presentations of the mainstream narrative. There is a market for whatever is most shocking, scandalous and counter-intuitive. So we have a significant section of the alternative media committed to adopting a contrary position on more or less everything.

Fifthly, a gulf has opened between mainstream media consumers and alternative media consumers, as each follows a more-of-the-same diet, made stricter still by social media algorithms that present even more more-of-the-same content.

Whichever camp we find ourselves in, or wherever we are along the spectrum, we need to be alert. Every issue needs assessing on its merits, regardless of our media preferences and habits.

Let's look at how this all plays out in practice. The Scottish Family Party has campaigned to draw attention to the government's dreadful sex education resources. One of our punchlines has been the absolutely justified claim that these lessons endorse pornography use. This is a classic case of a story circulated in alternative media (me, basically, with others echoing) that is not replicated in the mainstream media.

Some people are reluctant to believe so outlandish a claim. Surely it's an exaggeration. They can't really be the government's official resources. Schools would never actually teach that. Sometimes it starts sounding like sheer disbelief in the existence of evil within the political/educational establishment. If it's true, why hasn't it been covered in the mainstream media? Even when shown the indisputable sources, many still just don't want to leave the mainstream fold and adopt such an unorthodox position.

But others are only too keen to believe. It then becomes apparent that they believe a host of other unorthodox views. Trump really won the 2020 election. COVID 19 is a hoax. And that's just the start. I'm not going to discuss these particular beliefs, but what common thread runs through these disparate beliefs apart from active scepticism of the official mainstream narrative?

So what's my point? It seems that we each reside somewhere on the spectrum between uncritically gullible swallower of the mainstream narrative and compulsive conspiracy theorist. You may feel that you are the ideal hybrid of the two. Funny that; I think I am as well. Probably everyone does.

So what should we do? Do some people need to adopt a more critical stance towards the mainstream narrative? Do some need a pull back towards mainstream reality? These are tempting prescriptions, but wrong.

The ideal is to overcome our inclinations and prejudices by judging each case objectively on its own merits. Each side will claim to possess supportive facts, and these are probably true. But whose facts form the fullest picture? Which interpretation is most plausible? Critical assessment of competing views is hard work.

If your views are a combination of mainstream thought and alternative perspectives, you are probably avoiding the worst extremes of polarisation and thinking independently to some extent.

Currently, most Christians seem to tend towards credulity of the mainstream media narrative, despite its hostility to the Christian worldview. A minority have wandered into the land of wild conspiracy theories instead. We'll need our God-given wits about us to discern the truth on one issue after another.

SIN ≡ INJUSTICE?

Are you familiar with that symbol? In Mathematics it means "is identical to." If two terms are identical, then they are really just two different ways of expressing the same thing - not just that they may be equal on this particular occasion, but that they always have to be equal, because they are, effectively, the same thing.

There is a tacit belief abroad in Christendom that sin ≡ injustice. Every sin is an injustice and every injustice is a sin. If sin and injustice are really synonyms, then why not use the word that is currently in favour in our culture: injustice? Why not, indeed. If we can say what we need to say in terms that resonate with the wider public, we certainly should.

There is a serious caveat, though. Sin ≢ Injustice. Sin is not identical to injustice. Not every sin is an injustice and not every injustice is a sin.

Looking at a woman lustfully: is that an injustice? No. Is it a sin? Yes.

A referee fails to notice an attacker's handball when the winning goal is scored. The losing team has suffered an injustice. Has a sin been committed? No.

The overlap between sin and injustice is very broad indeed, but we will fall into errors if we treat them as the same thing.

A person from a Christian campaigning organisation recently said to me that to secure the interest of younger people, every issue has to be framed as an "injustice". Mere "evil" or "harmful" just don't cut through. "Injustice" is the key word.

That reflects a wider emphasis on injustice in political and cultural life. The classic illustration of this is the abhorrence that is elicited by sex-selective abortion - as it is manifestly "unjust" to kill

22

unborn children just because they are girls. That's sexism. That's injustice. But abortion in general is absolutely fine, apparently (as long as it is carried out equitably).

"Justice" is now associated closely with a definite left-leaning political philosophy that often involves the conflation of injustice with inequality. On this view, statistical differences between groups show inequality and therefore injustice, which needs government policy to tackle. I won't digress into a critique of this viewpoint. All we need to note here is that "justice" now has a distinct politicised meaning.

So, from a Christian point of view, not everything claimed as an injustice will necessarily be a violation of God's standards. We need to be discerning. Sure, the church should take a stand against injustice. But it should be injustice as defined in Christian teaching, not injustice as defined by political activists.

On the other hand, should we present our Christian principles in terms of justice and injustice where we can? Definitely.

In fact, let's go one step further. Let's start turning the tables and label elements of mainstream secular practice as injustices.

God is a God of justice, so we should be a people of justice, reflecting God's will.

CHRISTIAN VALUES OR CHRISTIAN IDENTITY?

What's more important, Christians in politics or Christian values in politics? Which is better: a Christian who does not stand up for what they believe, or an atheist or a Muslim holding the same values, who is willing to speak out and exert influence?

Our mission as Christians in politics is primarily to promote policies that reflect God's standards, wisdom and priorities and, therefore, contribute to the good of society. Any allies in this cause are welcome. Those hindering it are not allies, but opponents - whether they wear the Christian badge or not. Success is the advancement of righteous values in public debate and the implementation of such policies, whoever is involved.

It's always encouraging to hear of Christians in prominent positions. They can use their influence to portray the faith positively and demonstrate integrity in their field. The Christian footballer might make supporters more open to faith themselves, and his good conduct and sportsmanship can bear witness to his values (hopefully!). However, we don't need to care who he plays for, how many goals (or own goals) he scores, or how his team fares - winning the league is neither here nor there.

With politics, it's different. While a Christian politician might well bear witness to their personal faith effectively, it does matter which team they are on. We might not care who wins the league, but we do care when a political party enacts ungodly policies that will hurt individuals and fundamentally damage our society. Own goals in politics are not just embarrassing - a Christian politician whose actions result in anti-Christian policies advancing should not be cheered.

There is considerable scope for discussion of how Christian values are best promoted through the democratic system. I'm not ruling out any particular approach here. I'm just stating the objective.

The ultimate goal is not to have Christians in politics, but to have Christian values promoted in politics. So, on election day, the personal faith of individual politicians should count for little. We should vote for the values and policies we believe will benefit society.

Whether individual politicians wear the Christian badge or not should be of little consequence. We're not trying to advance our tribe at the expense of other identity groups, but to bring the fruit of righteousness into our national life.

JUST LOOKING AFTER OUR OWN?

Your kid's school is endorsing pornography and preaching values that will harm your children. What do you do? Priority: insulate your children from these messages. Withdraw them from sex education. What then? Warn other Christian parents and encourage them to do the same? OK, what then?

Sadly, for a lot of Christians, the answer seems to be nothing.

It's as if looking after our own children's education, supporting Christians in freedom of speech and conscience scrapes, and generally upholding Christian rights and freedoms is what it's all about.

I'm right behind every one of these things, but they should be a small subset of Christian political engagement.

Our mission in the world is much broader than just looking out for our own interests. Going back to the sex education, do we not care about all of the other children being misled and corrupted? The freedom of Christians to adhere to and articulate traditional teaching about marriage and family is vital, but surely a weightier issue still is the pain and lasting damage caused to countless in our society by a faulty understanding of sexual relationships and parenting?

As well as being more faithful to God's calling, showing ourselves to be concerned for the wellbeing of our whole society is far better PR. You might bristle at so worldly a consideration as Public Relations, but I'm not suggesting that Biblical principle be compromised to enhance the church's image. Quite the opposite. Expressing the fullness of God's will should enhance the credibility and attractiveness of the church, not diminish it. We don't want to be seen as yet another faction just looking after its own.

"WE SHOULDN'T IMPOSE OUR BELIEFS ON PEOPLE"

How often have you heard that? It's thrown into discussions as an absolute, often to near universal agreement. If there's one thing Christians seem to know about politics, it's that you shouldn't impose your views on people.

When it comes to religious doctrine, it's true. Not only is trying to coerce belief wrong, it's also impossible (you may be able to pressurise someone into submission, but it won't actually change what they believe) and pointless (the angels won't rejoice over the heretic frightened into external orthodoxy).

When it comes to morality, however, that's a different matter. Even the briefest analysis reveals that the "we mustn't impose our values" line doesn't hold water.

Here are two of my beliefs founded in Biblical teaching:

1) Murder is wrong
2) Adultery is wrong

Why are they wrong? Because they do harm and offend against God's moral standards - just like everything else that's morally wrong.

I assume all will agree that murder should be illegal. In other words, we are happy that our Christian morality is imposed by law in this case. Therefore, we actually believe that imposing our values on others can be justified.

The riposte at this point might be, "But everyone agrees that murder is wrong!" Again, a moment's reflection should dispel this objection. For a start, it's not true: sadly, there are those who do believe that murder is justified in their cause. Universal acceptance is not necessary when legislating, anyway. Not everyone agrees that taking heroin or driving at 100 mph should be illegal, but that is never taken as a knockdown argument against criminalising them.

So, we've got no qualms about imposing "Thou shalt not kill" through the law.

Let's move on to adultery, an evil that causes harm in society. Should it be illegal? Our nation has decided that it should not be a criminal offense. It is in some lands today (including several American states) and used to be here. You probably agree with me that prosecuting people for having an affair is not going to be helpful, so you don't want your Christian moral belief that adultery is wrong enshrining in criminal law.

My point here is this: there is no general rule that demands we always should or should not enact Christian moral teaching in law.

In addition, there is no general rule that demands that every action that is harmful to society should be illegal. Adultery is most definitely harmful and immoral, but we leave it largely outside the realm of the law.

So, we need to assess proposed laws and policies based on Christian moral principle individually, each on its own merits. The trite phrase "we shouldn't impose our beliefs on people" adds nothing to the discussion.

In politics, the aim is to make a better society. Political parties put forward policies that they believe will achieve this. If Christians believe that, say, maintaining the institution of marriage as being between a man and a woman would benefit society, they should feel entirely free to argue that. If promoting marriage would yield benefits in society, then seek to promote it. If you know that school lessons endorsing pornography contradict Jesus's ideal of sexual purity, then feel free to oppose them. It's not fundamentally different from any other policy proposal.

Let's remember that God's standards are not arbitrary but lead to better outcomes for all. And that's what politics is all about.

Does any other group enter the political fray holding that they ought not espouse their own values, or advocate measures reflecting them? I can't think of one. Christians seem unique in adopting this bizarre attitude of political self-elimination, while all-comers compete aggressively to mould policy and law in their own image.

The charge of "imposing beliefs" usually comes from secularists bent on eliminating perfectly valid religiously inspired views from political debate. We need not acquiesce.

"YOU CAN'T LEGISLATE FOR RIGHTEOUSNESS"

In Christian theology, righteousness can refer to a status before God. In that sense, certainly, the law of the land cannot produce righteousness and no one is claiming otherwise. Another wording making the same point is "you can't legislate the gospel." Again, while some Christians have erred in seeking to enforce faith legally in the past, such historical projects have no parallel in modern Scotland.

So, despite their irrelevance, these phrases are regularly trotted out as though they cut to the heart of Christian political engagement.

There is another (more practical but equally Biblical) meaning of righteousness, however. Righteousness can refer to moral character. Can contemporary legal codes produce moral character in those who are subject to them? Some would argue that refraining from bad behaviours out of fear of or respect for the law leaves a person's moral character unchanged.

I have two points to make in response. Firstly, I believe that the law can assist in personal moral formation. Secondly, even if it can't, the primary purpose of the law is to deter bad behaviour and thus protect citizens.

The habit of behaving legally, regardless of the motivation, can generate space for personal moral development. To use an extreme example, a man building his fortune on slavery will tend to be less open to the ideal that all humans are of equal worth and dignity. A man in a society where slavery is outlawed is more likely to embrace the ideal.

Less dramatically, in a land where corruption is effectively punished, qualities of honesty and integrity are likely to flourish.

As well as restraining the practice and habitualising of immoral behaviours, in a significant way the law acts as an expression of national morality. Therefore, good laws help underpin a strong moral culture in a society.

You might accept this argument or you might not, but I am going to say that the primary purpose of law is to restrain behaviour, not to mould character. I'd prefer a burglar to be deterred from breaking into my family home just because he fears punishment, than for him to conduct break-ins until he realises the error of his ways through sincere introspection. Laws primarily exist to protect from harm, not to develop virtue in the populace.

To use the example of abortion: the law can't make people respect the sanctity of human life, but it can save the lives of the unborn. And that's worth doing. So, we strive to save lives _and_ to change attitudes, recognising that progress with one will help with the other.

Unthinking sound bites like "you can't legislate for righteousness" imply that protecting people from harm by means of the law has no value. I don't see such disregard for human well-being in the character of God.

Something has gone very awry if we dismiss the promotion of the good of our fellow human beings as being beneath our spiritual calling.

"GOD IS IN CONTROL"

Is it God's will for Nicola Sturgeon to be the First Minister of Scotland? And Boris Johnson Prime Minister of the UK? Is it part of God's higher purpose that our current governments facilitate the killing of thousands of unborn children? Is it divine providence that has placed pornography promoters in charge of sex education in Scotland?

You may think that it is. Christians hold a range of views on God's determining and ordaining of worldly affairs - I'm not going to enter that debate here.

My concern is this. I have heard phrases such as "God is in control" used in a sense that implies endorsement of current political leaders and their policies. A further purported implication runs along the lines of "and so we shouldn't worry about it or seek to change things" - God is in control, after all.

So, even if we grant the most deterministic interpretation of God's sovereignty, what does it imply about our political engagement?

It might engender a sense of peace and reassurance that God is working out his purposes for the best, despite current challenges. But that's aside from our question: how should we engage in politics?

Here's the nub. If God has ordained that Nicola Sturgeon should be First Minister, does that mean that we shouldn't seek to remove her? If God had ordained that Hitler should be Chancellor of Germany, should Christians have just accepted his leadership? If God has ordained that the government implements evil policies, should we never seek to change them?

Surely God's plan can involve good people doing good things to bring about good outcomes, including replacing leaders who are leading us in a dark direction?

The way I see it is this: whether or not God has ordained that a certain political party holds power currently has no bearing whatsoever on whether or not we should seek to change it. I've never heard a Christian say to a doctor "it's God's will that people get ill, so you shouldn't interfere by trying to cure them." So why do those seeking political change for the better face the charge that they are somehow seeking to disrupt God's perfect pre-ordained plan? Well, I have no answer. It just seems completely illogical to single out politics as the one area where seeking the good of humanity is somehow unchristian.

Might the "don't bother with politics because God is in control" line be an excuse? Perhaps in some cases. If someone has no interest in politics and/or is averse to being seen to be going against the flow of society, a neat cover-all get out clause might be attractive.

Allowing evil to flourish unopposed should not be a consequence of faith in God's sovereignty. It is an abdication of Christian responsibility.

PART 2

UNMUFFLING THE PROPHETIC VOICE

NICENESS

Political debate is robust. Attacking the policies, wisdom and competence of political opponents is an inevitable and even necessary aspect of democratic government.

Many Christians seem happy to support mainstream politicians who are robust in their critique of the "other side", attacking alternative policies and their proponents with little restraint. We hope for a degree of civility, but democratic political discourse will rightly involve direct criticism of competitors.

In contrast, individual Christians more often find themselves discussing their beliefs in informal conversation. Stridency would be inappropriate in this context. Building relationships and exploring different perspectives sensitively is the order of the day.

When it comes to articulating Christian truth in the political realm, many Christians apply the standards of personal evangelism and frown on the bold assertion of Biblical principle. To criticise a party or politician for their immoral policies or views is seen as somehow unchristian and not very nice.

This double standard can be stark. When mainstream politicians use the most florid and uncharitable terms over mainstream political issues ("shameful" seems the current favourite), Christians usually take no exception. But, for example, when someone talks straight about the evil of killing unborn children, they can become distinctly uncomfortable, suggesting that niceness or wisdom demand euphemistic sensitivity.

This misplaced reticence to make our case directly and strongly weakens our voice. An atmosphere of distaste for bold assertion of Christian truth deters Christians from even seeking to enter debate. Those doing so regardless fear "friendly fire incidents" as much as they expect encouragement.

There is plenty of Biblical justification, from the Prophets to Jesus Himself, for forthright, provocative and contentious communication that runs the risk of inflaming opponents.

Christians need not contend with one hand tied behind their back. The priority isn't always to gently persuade opponents, sometimes it's to expose evil and mobilise opposition.

Christians should be supportive of the promotion of Christian values in politics by the means that they endorse for all other political issues. There is no reason to soft-pedal on the weightiest matters.

"IF WE SPEAK THE TRUTH, IT MIGHT PUT PEOPLE OFF COMING TO THE CAROL SERVICE."

What is the church for? Evangelism is a major component of the mission of the local church and denominations.

Some people bitterly resent and oppose the church's teaching in some peripheral areas. So, best not talk about those and hope people come to the church and become Christians. Then we can bring up other teachings later.

That's the tacit philosophy of many churches. There are two problems with it.

1) The responsibility of the church to promote and defend righteousness in society can't be overlooked. What would we say to a church in 1805 that didn't like to say anything about slavery because it was controversial and might put some people off coming to the church? And a church now that fails to speak up for the thousands of unborn children being killed?

    Evangelistic ambition does not absolve us of our responsibility to the vulnerable, the needy and the mistreated.

    "Speaking up on behalf of the unborn doesn't really fit with our church marketing strategy currently." Is that a bit too close to actuality for comfort?

2) God's truth resonates with people's God-given conscience. However negative their outwards reaction, we should

believe that truth has power. While the truth may repel some, it will simultaneously challenge them. The truth will attract others. There is a values vacuum in our society; people are seeking solid ground. Self-less campaigning shows the church as principled and committed.

Is there any evidence that presenting a less challenging message enhances evangelistic effectiveness? Doesn't the evidence indicate the opposite?

The church needs to have confidence in God's standards. If we present our case, it's coherence and wisdom will be apparent to the open-minded.

If the church fails to take to the field, the game still carries on. Every soul in the land is subject to a deluge of messages that contradict Biblical standards. Does that really produce the most fertile ground for the gospel?

RICHARD LUCAS

SPEAKING THE TRUTH IN LOVE

When it comes to public communication, if there's one phrase lodged in the minds of Christians it's this: we must speak the truth in love.

Many, if not most, Christians, churches and denominations seem so concerned about the "in love" bit that they never do the "speaking the truth" bit. But that's not my point here.

What does it mean to speak the truth in love?

I'll start by dismissing a few red herrings: always having a benign smile and soft voice, always addressing individuals rather than generalities, always making emotional response the central concern, constant apology for any offense or hurt caused, or just general timidity and dilution of challenging messages.

Calling out evil as evil is sometimes exactly what's needed (though some Christians seem to lack the stomach for it).

I haven't got a strict definition to offer, but I have landed on these guides:

1) Show consideration for the effects of what you are saying on individuals. The message can still be clear and direct, but the challenge it represents to some can be acknowledged and addressed when appropriate.

2) Don't ascribe malice lightly. Politicians are often just driven along by winds of fashion rather than knowingly promoting harmful ideologies. That's still blameworthy, but it is different. Similarly, incompetence, ignorance and cowardice are not corruption, malevolence and conspiracy. The language should not overreach reality.

As the trend to claim that political opponents "should be locked up" is seeping over from America, we must be more temperate and factual.

3) Refrain from personally insulting language (though pointing out character flaws may be necessary).

4) Don't steal people's dignity. Treat people respectfully. In a recent election campaign, the Scottish National Party (SNP) produced leaflets showing just the top of Boris Johnson's head - that's undignified. Similarly, the old Conservative posters showing Blair with demonic eyes were out of order. Even using a deliberately selected unflattering photograph is questionable. Disparaging nicknames and attacks on appearance etc. should be avoided.

5) As Jesus said, don't call people fools. There are times when I diagnose the problem with, say, an MSP is that they lack the IQ required to grasp the arguments put to them. However, I endeavour to refrain from directly questioning intellectual capability, though I may comment on a particular situation where someone does not seem to be understanding. There have also been times when politicians have said things so foolish as to be literally laughable. While I might report, I try not to laugh. I might have done in the past, but I try not to now.

There will always be grey areas and disagreements in this area, but God knows the heart, and we should love all.

By showing this restraint, are we laying down some effective weapons? No. I often imagine keyboard warriors who fire off salvos of, to say the least, uncharitable remarks sitting back in their chair and congratulating themselves on a job well done. A blow struck for their cause. That's told them! But all that has really been achieved is the alienation of more moderate potential supporters and the reinforcement of opponents in their beliefs.

A final word to Christian leaders, who might feel these tensions most acutely. How do you preach moral truth with love? Well, the answer is simple. Do it like God does. Uphold moral standards while holding out the offer of forgiveness, restoration and relationship. It's the perfect formula. Those of us in the political arena can't bring in the Christian gospel alongside every pronouncement, but Christian leaders can.

If the message of the gospel has been reduced to "Come to Jesus and He'll help you with your emotional needs," then tacking on weighty moral teaching is going to jar. But the gospel is "Repent and be saved," so awareness of sins is a part of God's loving plan of salvation.

How can we preach the truth in love? Maybe that's the wrong question. Perhaps a more apposite question is can we really preach love without the truth?

"WE NEED TO BE KNOWN FOR WHAT WE'RE FOR, NOT WHAT WE'RE AGAINST!"

"St Peter's Church stands against the killing of the unborn."

The chorus would swell across Christendom: "I wish they wouldn't say that. It's so negative. We want the church to be known for what we're FOR not what we're AGAINST."

"St Peter's Church stands against racism."

Would anyone reply "I wish they wouldn't say that. It's so negative. We want the church to be known for what we're FOR not what we're AGAINST"? Never.

It is clear that when people say the church should be positive not negative, what they really mean is that the church should stick to uncontroversial moral issues and remain silent on contentious ones – the one's where the church's voice is most needed.

What is really meant is "We need to be known for being for or against exactly the same things that the mainstream of society is for or against."

As if one fatal flaw in this line were not enough, there is a second. Every stance can be expressed as a positive or a negative.

Against racism or for racial equality?

Against abortion or pro-life?

Against uncommitted sexual relationships or pro-marriage?

Against euthanasia or for valuing every human life?

Sometimes the positive or the negative is the more succinct and accurate articulation, but is there really a fundamental gulf between positivity and negativity?

Of course, a positive tone and emphasis might be more attractive but, ultimately, we must oppose what's wrong and commend what's right.

We need to be known for being for goodness and against evil. If we care about people more than we care about our reputation, there's no other way.

WISDOM, FEARFULNESS AND SELF-INTEREST

We live in strange times. Parroting the fashionable consensus view is often lauded as "brave." Expressing an alternative view, in the face of hostility, is generally regarded as distasteful, at least.

The benefits of staying within the borders of acceptable opinion can be great: smooth career progression, social acceptance, approval and public profile. Deviating can be very costly.

But, as Jordan Peterson points out, you pay a price either way. The price paid by those who speak out is often clear. The price paid by the silent can be more subtle and insidious. Loss of self-respect. Guilt. Lack of purpose. Compromised character. Over a lifetime, these are serious costs.

Keeping silent where you know there is a desperate need for the truth is habit forming. Once one starts down the road of compromise and self-censorship, it can be very difficult to break out of it. It seems that those choosing this route usually follow it progressively throughout their careers. Usually those "waiting for the right time to speak out" seem to wait forever.

That's not to say that everyone needs to speak up about every issue that arises on every opportunity, in the most forthright terms. The danger is that routine restraint to the point of silence can be habit forming. In our context it is easy to mistake fearfulness and self-interest for wisdom.

The "wisdom" of silence is infectious. As more commend themselves and others for it, more will be drawn in.

I realised many years ago that my teaching career was not destined to end with retirement. Not if I kept articulating

Christian truth publicly, anyway. My decision was to accept the right of my employer and professional body to instruct me about the performance of my duties (even if I thought their policies misguided), but to defy any restrictions relating to my writing, speaking and debating outside any professional context. It was liberating to be free from seemingly endless negotiation, compromise and pressure. The ball was no longer in my court.

In taking such a stance, one must face the possible consequences, but maybe those waving the guns so threateningly will ultimately be reluctant to pull the trigger. We might be delivered from the fiery furnace. Or new and exciting opportunities might be realised once we are forced to look beyond the comfortable status quo. That's one the reason why the persecution of the church has so often backfired. Deprive Christians of their employment and, lo and behold, more and more commit more and more time to Christian ministry.

The more people speak up with a controversial view, the harder it is to demonise it. There is strength, and safety, in numbers.

Let's remember that what we're talking about here isn't just winning the right to do what we want to do, against the objections of others. It's not like wanting to smoke in the staff dining room. It's about promoting the wellbeing of our society and protecting individuals from serious harm.

Everyone's situation is different, embedded in a certain set of relationships and fulfilling a distinct calling, but ultimately, we need to speak the truth and face the consequences.

PSYCHOLOGY

One of the five key personality traits measured by psychologists is agreeableness. A more agreeable person will like to smooth things over and maintain harmony. Put them in a discussion with ten other people and they are unlikely to rock the boat with an unpopular viewpoint. Better to just keep quiet and keep those delicate relationships intact.

The less agreeable might be more willing to disturb the comfortable collegiality by throwing in a contrary perspective. The more agreeable might bemoan the intervention as spoiling the previously nice atmosphere.

Go further along the range of personalities and eventually get to people like me, who are delighted to have the opportunity to create real debate, challenge the unanimity and say what really needs saying. It's not that we don't care what people think or don't value relationships, it's just that sitting listening to a discussion where absolutely key factors are being neglected is excruciating! We want to help people understand, even if they don't want to!

So, is there an ideal degree of agreeableness? No. The perpetual doormat and perpetually contrary illustrate dangers at the extremes, but, in between, it takes all sorts, as the saying goes.

In my teaching days each term was preceded by about two days of training, with perhaps four sessions per day. The "experts" brought in to share their wisdom often instead shared pseudo-scientific drivel ("Massaging the neck increases blood flow to the brain and enhances Maths performance") and fashionable educational ideology ("Every pupil can achieve an A Level Maths A grade with the right support").

There might be five for six times during a day when I'd be

itching to put up my hand and challenge, but people don't want to hear too much from one person. It could be seen as a bit impolite to expose visiting "experts" as charlatans. The school leaders might not appreciate it being made too explicit that they repeatedly pay for very dubious ideas to be shared with staff. So, I made myself a rule: only two interjections per day permitted. Did it work? Maybe, partially, but I was still the most independently thinking/awkward teacher by far!

We each approach politics as who we are, with our own personality. Some prefer harmonious consensus, some prefer rigorous and challenging debate. Whatever our personality, we have to weigh up the best course of action in any scenario.

Do you want to really get to know your local MSP and develop a positive relationship? Is your strategy to overlook the sins of his party and even his own immoral viewpoints in order to get the opportunity to drop into a friendly chat a nugget of Christian wisdom? Or is your mission to expose sinful policies and renounce his immoral viewpoints. Perhaps there is a middle path to seek as well, but it is very precarious.

My point is that your personality will be a strong driver of your subjective preference between these approaches. However, we also need to bring in an objective element to our thinking. The further policies deviate from righteousness and truth, the stronger the imperative to challenge them overtly and publicly.

If you are a more agreeable type, you might not really want to hear about the grave immorality of various party policies, preferring to maintain a stance of benevolent mutual good-will. People are going to get upset if you start spelling out where they are wrong - very wrong.

On the other hand, those with low levels of agreeableness

need to beware of the temptation to place the worst possible construction on every government policy, seeing malignancy where there is really only disagreement. This can be the road to unjustified conspiracy theorising.

Where are we today in Scotland? The centre of political policy has veered into sheer immorality in several areas. I won't rattle off a list again, but you know some of the areas I mean. I suggest, therefore, that those of a rather less agreeable disposition might find it easier to respond. The agreeable might find the tension too uncomfortable.

We don't get to choose the age we live in. We've landed in a context where evils are being enacted as public policy. We each must, on occasion, set aside our desire for harmony and universal acceptance and speak the truth.

SOCIOLOGY

Where do you want to be positioned in society?

We don't care for such things as Christians, of course. We live out our calling in whatever station, humble or exalted, is appointed to us in the divine plan.

Well, that's the theory, anyway.

Unless you are in a particularly advanced state of sainthood, you will actually quite like projecting a certain personal image. When you tell people what you do, where you live, what you drive or who you know, you might feel either a flicker of pride or a wince of embarrassment. Would that such worldly considerations were swept from our minds, but our perfection lies in the future still.

How about for a church leader? Are you the sort that is an important figure in the community, rubbing shoulders with other local leaders - including politicians? Is that your stratum in society? Do you quite like the feeling of mixing with the elite?

Reaching out to all, including the "great and the good" is admirable and beneficial, but might a slither of pride lead us to prioritise familiarity with the prominent and powerful at the expense of upholding the truth?

An intelligent politician will hold out a hand of friendship to anyone who'll refrain from stern critique. That may be a great deal for the politician, but is it for the Christian?

How many Christians have gained prominence, circulated in exalted circles, earned the plaudits of the cultural mainstream, then, slowly but surely diluted their faith and principles? The wording becomes ever more qualified and cautious. Silence follows. Then comments start betraying a wholly different world view. The hopes of the faithful are dashed yet again.

The ability to "fit in" with those advocating evil might have its advantages, but it's certainly got its dangers as well.

Further Reading: the gospels, especially the words of Jesus.

FIRST THEY CAME FOR THE...

First they came for the eccentric street preacher who was, frankly, an embarrassment to the church, so we didn't openly support him.

Then they came for the church who invited an abrasive speaker who we wouldn't have invited, so we didn't openly support them.

Then they came for the nurse who prayed with a patient when asked to, but that's a bit of a grey area, so we didn't openly support her.

Then they came for the social worker who defended traditional marriage on social media, but we didn't like the way he phrased it, so we didn't openly support him.

Then they came for the teacher in our church who said that homosexual sex is immoral. Other people in the church were a bit twitchy in case they were associated with this view, so we didn't support him openly.

Then they came for us. And the rest of Christendom saw that we were the perfect embodiment of Godly wisdom in every way, so they all rallied round and openly supported us.

Dream on.

If you really think that a Christian has made a mistake in the way they acted or communicated, let them know. Try to take into account that their context is probably very different to a speaker in a church, and that there is not always time or attention span to dispel every possible misinterpretation before delivering the punchline. Those of us on the front line should be ready to listen, reflect and learn. Those advising should be mindful of their likely lack of experience in the field.

The most important thing, though, is to support them, both behind the scenes and publicly. In my experience, messages of encouragement and support have been invaluable and appreciated.

When you are feeling like the whole media and establishment is against you, however, what you crave is people and organisations standing alongside you expressing support publicly. For some time I have committed to being public in my support of any Christian facing mistreatment on account of their faith, and the Scottish Family Party similarly will back those whose freedom of speech and conscience is under threat.

Wherever possible, that support should be unequivocal, focussing on the heart of the issue: controversial Biblical teaching.

If we were all in the habit of standing up for each other, everyone who paid a price for speaking the truth would find a crowd standing with them. That's the way it should be.

And, who knows, those contemplating taking a swipe at the next Christian to transgress secular orthodoxy might just think again. Do they really want to be swamped with social media criticism? A demonstration in front of their building? Do they want their receptionists fielding difficult calls for the next week? Might be easier to just let it slide. Christian freedom would be defended for all.

More importantly, the world would see a united church, committed to Godly principles and to each other.

First they came for…..

and they immediately found themselves confronted by a united church standing firmly in solidarity.

Now there's a dream to pursue.

CHRISTIAN LANGUAGE

Christians in the nations in a season such as this often feel led to share what's on their heart in quite distinctive language. However, there is a time and a place for everything.

Politics is about policy. Policy is about improving people's lives. So we should argue for policies on that basis. Now I believe that God's moral standards do indeed maximise human well-being, but I urge public policy on the basis of this utility, not on religious grounds.

Does one arguing for a policy because it reflects their religious beliefs deserve their voice to be heard? Of course. Are they likely to persuade anyone outside their religious circle? No.

If we argue on the basis of what works, we'll find a broad coalition of allies aligning with us, and others may be persuaded by the case made.

The theological underpinnings of our beliefs are not an embarrassing secret to bury out of sight, though. We can be open about them, as individuals, as means of demonstrating personal integrity and sharing our beliefs.

How about the more florid end of Christian language?

At First Minister's Question Time, should a Member of the Scottish Parliament ask the First Minister, "Do you agree that abortion is an abomination before God? It is nothing short of Satanic. The Government needs to repent and turn the nation back to God's Word"? What effect would this have? It could alienate a majority who are a million miles from the worldview behind it. It would attract ridicule. It could cement people in their pro-abortion stance as they are confirmed in their belief that the pro-life side comprises religious fanatics. And, who knows, it might bring conviction and repentance.

As a matter of routine, however, I believe it is best to present arguments that seek to build on common assumptions and available facts. Most politicians would be more uncomfortable explaining why they don't value all human life than denying conspiracy with the Devil.

If we want to persuade those who don't yet agree, unite those who already agree, put opponents on the back foot, and promote the truth in public debate, it's usually best to leave explicitly Christian language in the background. Not buried, but in the background.

Then, who knows, when people's God given conscience resonates with our words, they'll notice that it's often Christians speaking the sense and the truth. They might want to start to explore why.

MEN

Does your conception of Christian manhood stop at manning the BBQ at the church picnic?

We live in a feminised society. Traits associated with femininity are honoured while masculine qualities are demonised. There is a tacit, or not so tacit, assumption that women are that little bit superior to men and that men could improve by being a bit more typically feminine.

In consequence, relational, therapeutic and empathic approaches are routinely commended. Confrontational, bold and principled stances are not really flavour of the century.

Yes, yes, yes. I know that these are generalisations and there is value in all approaches and some women... and some men...., but I'm just saying that the balance has tipped in a decidedly feminine direction.

This cultural trend is reflected in the church. It started in the 1990s with male preachers starting to explicitly contrast wise women with foolish men in the Bible. While believing that they were being humble in denigrating their own sex, they were in fact contrasting unreformed men with enlightened men such as themselves, or so they thought. In step with secular culture, it progressed from there.

Do we now assume that everyone's greatest need is emotional support? Help through the difficulties of life?

"Jesus can help you through this time when you're feeling low." Great message.

"There's a battle between good and evil going on and you need to get on the front line and play your part fighting it!" Great message.

Which do you hear more of? Which might appeal more to men or to women, generally?

Where does the calling into politics fit in? Even if political or campaigning action is advocated, what ideal form will be presented? Bold assertion of the truth? Overt challenge of evils? Or quietly building relationships and softly questioning? Again, there is a place for both, but the fruit of an unbalanced church will be unbalanced political engagement. And many men's natural desire and even calling to enter the fray with a steely determination in their hearts to protect the innocent might be frowned upon.

Sometimes evil needs to be named and condemned, and resistance mobilised. How many men feel the stirrings of calling in this direction, but dismiss it as somehow unchristian, instead living out their days in therapeutic small groups, struggling to master the sound desk, and manning the BBQ at the church picnic.

PART 3

DEMOCRATIC INFLUENCE: USE IT OR LOSE IT!

NEWSFLASH: WE LIVE IN A DEMOCRACY!

Many Christians seem to have philosophies of political engagement that neglect the fact that we live in a democracy. Why is this?

The Bible presents three distinct types of political or governmental involvement. Firstly, there are Old Testament rulers over God's people appointed by God. Then there are divinely placed political insiders exerting Godly influence. Finally, the prophetic outsiders inject truth from the margins. Democratic processes play no part for the simple reason that no democratic societies feature in the Biblical narrative.

These models can lead Christians to overlook the democratic possibility of putting prophets into positions of prominence by deliberately voting for them. "Join a mainstream party and hope to get elected" is the assumed route to Christian representation in parliament. Or speak prophetically from the sidelines. Voting for a party that represents Christian values is not usually considered.

This leaves many Christians voting on the basis of mainstream political issues, then feeling that many of their core values are unrepresented in political debate. Then they might campaign and write to their MSP about their concerns, but the vast majority of MSPs and certainly the parties are unreceptive. Even if the individual MSP is more in agreement, the direction of party and government policy remains unchanged.

By this strategy, Christians fail to register their distinctive views through the democratic process. It's election day that determines the political direction of the nation. And it's election day when many Christians take a day off from political action inspired by their distinctive values.

This neglect of the democratic system can be compounded by Christian charities. Many groups that campaign to promote Christian values in the political arena are registered charities, so they must be careful not to endorse any particular party. So what sort of activity can they encourage? Writing to elected politicians, signing petitions and the like. Anything, really, apart from voting for a party that will actually advance their agenda in parliament. They can congratulate and give a platform to representatives of parties completely at odds with their core values, but presenting a party sharing their core values is taboo.

The current Holyrood parties are satisfied with this state of affairs. They cannot afford to split their vote by taking a distinct line on controversial moral issues even if they wanted to. The last thing they want is Christian moral values entering mainstream political debate. They want to ignore them or contradict them without fear of electoral consequence. Sending a few bland letters to challenging constituents is a small price to pay to keep Christian values where they think they belong: on the sidelines.

Imagine this: instead of forming the SNP, Scottish nationalists had invested their energies in writing strongly worded letters to Labour and Conservative politicians urging them to embrace the cause of independence. Where would that have got them? Nowhere. Instead, they had the sense to form a party embodying their core values and enter the political fray - at the ballot box - despite the initial odds being stacked against them.

How many Christians cycle through this sequence?

1) Vote for a mainstream party that doesn't represent their core values.
2) Spend the next four years complaining that their views are not represented in Parliament.

3) Return to step 1.

It's time to break the cycle.

Election day should not be a holiday from Christian political engagement. It is the day when we have real power at our fingertips. Let's use it.

THE LESSER OF A FEW EVILS?

When no party represents one's views on critical moral values, is it best to vote for the lesser of two (or more) evils? Possibly, but it depends on the particular context and what is at stake.

To make my point I'll use an extreme illustration: if the choice was just between Party A promising to kill all Jews and Party B promising only to kill half of them, which would you vote for? One could attempt to justify a vote for Party B on utilitarian grounds because it leads to fewer deaths. But can you, in good conscience, express support for Party B by voting for them? Could you, as a Christian, be a member of Party B and thereby align yourself with it? At election time, could you knock on doors and implore people to vote for party B?

How about joining Party A in order to influence it from the inside? That might be a noble end, but in doing so you are expressing public support for Party A, contributing to them financially, and implying that you think that others should vote for them as well. Even if you are vocal in opposition to their murderous policy, your membership of the party implies that you do not see Jew killing as a deal breaker. That is surely unconscionable. The same argument applies to Party B.

So, in this case, starting/supporting a new party is the only acceptable option.

However, if existing parties do not espouse policies that directly contravene God's moral standards on weighty issues, then voting for, joining or supporting one might be a valid option, possibly with the intention of exerting influence within it.

So, which category do the Holyrood parties fall into? To begin, I suggest we bring to mind the 13,500 abortions in Scotland each year that proceed with the tacit or enthusiastic approval of all Holyrood parties. We believe that abortion involves the taking of innocent human life. Should that be a dealbreaker for Christians?

Can you support a party that is perfectly willing to see thousands of human lives deliberately ended? If you can, then you are making a very clear statement that the preservation of human life is not a non-negotiable principle for you. Can you seriously claim to see abortion as a matter of life and death while endorsing the parties endorsing the killing?

One argument against this principled position could run like this: if you vote for a party with a chance of winning, at least you'll have had some influence. Two points can be made in reply. Firstly, there is no such thing as a wasted vote. All parties look at election results and learn. If they see votes for small parties with different moral outlook than their own, they realise that there are voters who are put off by their current stance - voters who might be won over by changing it. Every additional vote counted for a party embodying your moral values has an influence.

The most powerful argument here is more simple, though. We are in Scotland. Small parties can see representatives elected for as little as 5% on the Regional List system. There are more than enough people with strong values.

t's time to face up to the cold hard logic: membership of, support for, or even a vote for the SNP, Labour, Lib Dems, Greens or the Conservatives implies that industrial scale killing of the unborn is not a deal breaker for you.
It took me a long time to arrive at this conclusion, but perhaps you can accept the truth more quickly, if you haven't already.

A helpful way of clarifying our thinking can be to replace a word with an accurate alternative, so, if you want to test your resolution to resist the implication of supporting a pro-abortion party, try standing in front of the mirror and saying a few lines like this:

"I voted for a party that wants to continue the killing of unborn children because they were the ones most likely to beat the SNP here."

"I am a member of a party that wants to allow the killing of unborn children right up to birth because I am concerned about climate change."

"I urge you to vote for a party that wants even more unborn children to be killed, because Scotland should be an independent nation."

If your conscience allows you to say these things in good faith, well, at least you have faced up to actuality. If it doesn't, it's time for a shift in your political allegiance.

FRIENDS OR ENEMIES?

The consensus among Christians seems to run a bit like this: you can be a Christian in any political party – choosing a party is a matter of personal political taste, not Christian principle. Christians in all parties then enjoy a degree of fellowship and they might even work together on some issues of conscience promoting a Biblical view.

So, Sam in the SNP will disagree with Carol of the Conservatives about independence, Brexit and the economy. But what if SNP Sam completely fails to speak out on behalf of the unborn, and Conservative Carol stays silent as transgender indoctrination is rolled out into schools? Should they criticise each other? Or would that seem somehow disloyal? A friendly fire incident?

Let's imagine Sam and Carol are candidates in the same constituency and face each other in the local church hustings. A question is asked, "Would you speak up on behalf of the unborn?" "I have and I will," answers Sam, "unlike Carol, who has always remained silent on the issue." Would Sam win support from the church audience? Or are they more likely to be drawn towards Carol out of sympathy? Would Sam be regarded as a touch nasty for criticising his Christian sister in this way? Very possibly.

So, here's the question. Should Christian solidarity extend to precluding open criticism of other Christians for their failure to speak up? Is questioning their personal commitment to, say, the environmental cause fine, but questioning their commitment to the pro-life cause somehow out of order? If so, why? Is the green cause more important?

If Christians feel restrained from pointing out the silence of other Christian politicians on key moral issues, doesn't that partially eliminate those issues from the democratic process? How can the more outspoken commend themselves to the electorate in contrast to the more compromised? The electorate cannot be relied upon to follow political debate closely enough to notice the difference for themselves.

Enough of the questions. What are my answers?

I generally don't criticise individual Christian politicians for their failures to stand up and speak out, though I will make general statements of the "not a single MSP has…" form. Why don't I call out individuals? Partly because I think it would alienate Christians imbued with the "friendly fire" philosophy. But that's not the whole story. Something in me does baulk at criticising another Christian in politics. It could be because I have met several of them and appreciate the pressures and restraints under which they operate, and know how they struggle with these. I also believe that I would be more outspoken in their shoes. I also know that I would never be in their shoes because their parties would not accept a representative as outspoken as me. But then my sympathy is eroded by the thought that they chose to enter their current party knowing full well that severe self-censorship would be required.

So, yes, I do feel restrained from publicly criticising other Christian politicians, and that restraint stems in part from a sense of Christian solidarity.

When it comes to their wayward parties and their gravely immoral policies, however, it's open season!

PS. I have no qualms whatsoever criticising those politicians who claim Christian faith or church membership while explicitly espousing values at odds with Biblical teaching.

FOR A CANDIDATE NOT A PARTY

If no party embodies Christian values, how about voting for the best candidate? At least that might secure one vote and one voice for righteousness in the parliament? It might do, but the elected representative might backtrack when under the pressures of party, media and political culture.

Even if they are true to their colours, the main effect of your vote is to endorse their party, and possibly make it the government.

Parties can cleverly place Christian candidates in areas where they fear that Christian views may be more common. By this tactic, they can keep Christian voters on board while steering a course in an anti-Christian direction.

What can be done if a Christian MP or MSP is deserving of a more prominent role? The usual strategy seems to be to give them responsibilities well away from contentious moral issues. Finance, constitution, transport - they're pretty safe bets. Education? Equality? Human Rights? Best keep them well clear of these areas or their Christian values might start "interfering" with their role.

The emphasis on finding candidates' personal views can be justified if politics remains a competition between parties that don't promote distinctive Christian moral values. But what happens when a party that does make such principles a matter of policy enters the fray?

Christian voters are deciding which party or candidate to vote for. They might be influenced by Christian MSPs in the current Holyrood parties, and also consider the Scottish Family Party. Their thoughts might run along the lines that a lovely Christian

MSP goes to the church down the road and appears at Christian events, and the SFP seems to have Christian principles.

Is there a danger that the existing Christian MSPs are inducing Christians to vote for parties that utterly reject some of their core beliefs? While they might exert some positive influence within their party, might the net effect be negative as they garner the Christian vote for parties with policies that severely infringe Christian moral teaching?

That's an open question.

MATTERS OF CONSCIENCE

There is a tradition in UK politics that some moral issues are treated as "matters of conscience" by political parties. This (allegedly) removes some moral issues like abortion and assisted suicide from the realm of party politics, leaving individual elected representatives to vote as their conscience dictates (or, in many cases, as the winds of fashion blow).

This tradition may protect the freedom of conscience of the politicians, but the exclusion of key issues from manifestos and party campaigning disenfranchises the electorate.

Declaring an issue like abortion to be a matter of conscience amounts to telling the electorate that they can't use their vote to influence it. Even if one votes for a candidate who is pro-life, for example, and they win, their party will not permit them to prioritise the issue and take a Wilberforce style leadership role to bring about change.

As long as such issues are kept out of manifestos, they are kept out of election campaign debates and the illusion is created that they are not "real" political topics, but just side issues suitable for specific lobbying and campaigning. By this side-lining, the precipitous slide into progressivism proceeds unopposed.

The actual function of "matters of conscience" ploy is to keep those holding traditional Christian values (for example) within the fold, either as an elected representative or, by extension, as voters.

Let's take an example. The Conservative Party is a pro-abortion party. Most of their representatives are pro-abortion and they make no moves in the pro-life direction when in power. However, the fact that they don't declare this as an explicit policy position means that their pro-life members can, frankly, kid themselves that their party is somehow neutral on the matter, thus salving their consciences.

It's time to face the facts. A party that is not explicitly pro-life is functionally pro-abortion. An issue rises up the political agenda as more people begin to base their voting decision on it. Christians need to stop being fobbed off with the "matter of conscience" line.

"Please vote for a party that condones the killing of unborn children because they do let you stay in the party even if you disagree." How's that sound?

There's another way to understand a "matter of conscience": a matter where a fundamental moral principle is at stake. A matter of such gravity that a principled stand is demanded. A matter on which conscience dictates that compromise is unacceptable.

Politics needs more people for whom a "matter of conscience" is an inviolable principle, not an excuse to compromise on their core values.

WHY NOT A CHRISTIAN PARTY?

No one is representing our Christian values in Parliament. Surely we need a Christian Party to do just that? Isn't that how democracy is supposed to work? Especially where there is a degree of proportional representation?

Sounds sensible - apart from eight serious objections!

1. Politics should be about policy not identity. Political parties should offer voters policies, a plan to run the country, not identity alignment. Placing religious identity front and centre leads to a neglect of policy analysis by voters. Also, metaphysical religious beliefs have no direct impact on political policy. It is a religion's moral and social teaching that is relevant, and this is rarely unique to one religion.

2. Christians disagree on core moral issues. We might question the faith of some as they contradict every principle of traditional Christian moral teaching, but the fact is that a "Christian Party" will always have a queue of Christians or "Christians" coming to deny that it is truly Christian. While such internal tensions within Christendom may be of great import, exposing them in the political arena achieves little beyond discrediting the church.

3. Christians disagree on other political matters. Some Christians want a higher tax rate, some lower. Neither can claim indisputable divine sanction for their opinion. So, what does a Christian Party do? Refrain from all

policy areas where Biblical teaching is not decisive? That will leave huge gaps in the manifesto to say the least. But if positions are taken, these automatically appear under the "Christian" banner. This alienates Christians who disagree and misleads others into thinking that the debatable policy is actually orthodox Christian teaching.

4) If people are encouraged to vote according to religious identity then political divides become irreconcilable. Where is the middle ground between Christian, Muslim and atheist parties? How does a Muslim party seek to win over Christian voters? Religious identity politics is the scourge of many a nation, often descending into civil war.

5 God's standards are imprinted onto the conscience of all, so why reduce potential support by slicing the portion of the electorate who hold to these truths? Seeking to divide the socially conservative pie into religious slices will often lead to the electoral failure of each. The world situation demonstrates this effect. The liberal/ progressive/secular movement is united worldwide. The socially conservative/traditional/religious forces are fragmented into religious groupings. That's one reason why the liberal/progressive/secular side dominates at the UN, for example. Let's not replicate the same problem domestically.

6 If an explicitly Christian party gains power, to what extent can it govern even-handedly on behalf of all citizens? Even if it can, it will be well-nigh impossible to persuade others that this is the case, fermenting resentment and inviting other identity groups to seek to grasp the reins.

7 If a Christian party governs, its successes and failures will reflect on the church. That is a heavy responsibility to bear. When it is removed from power it will be seen as a defeat for Christianity. Nations such as Germany which have parties with "Christian" in their name do not experience this phenomenon because these parties have long since lost any mooring in Christian teaching and are no longer regarded as Christian in any meaningful sense.

8 A Christian party in power or getting representatives elected will attract the ambitious. The inevitable temptation will emerge to pretend Christian faith to gain access to the opportunity of a political career. This dishonesty will systematically weaken and sporadically embarrass the party.

These are weighty objections, but I would vote, in fact I have voted, for a Christian party. When weighed against the critical moral failing of the mainstream political parties, these objections are less serious. I applaud the efforts of those who have sought to bring Christian values into politics through Christian parties, but there is a better way.

THE BIGGER PICTURE

Lacking their own moral compass, many domestic politicians are never happier than when doing as they are told by supranational entities. And it is often the opposite of what The Supernatural Entity requires.

The United Nations, through its various agencies and committees, exhorts, cajoles and pressurises nations to comply with its will. Its will is often beneficent, but not always. The UN has a clear progressive/secular bias.

The same could be said of the EU.

When the familiar questions of gender, family, sexuality, sex education, abortion etc. are addressed by the UN, the conclusion is almost always the opposite of traditional Christian teaching. And traditional Muslim teaching. And traditional Hindu teaching. And traditional Sikh teaching. And traditional Buddhist teaching.

Are moral conservatives a minority of the world's population? Does the UN's stance reflect the majority? No and No.

So how does a minority dominate at the UN? The best explanation I've heard is this: moral conservatives are divided into mutually suspicious religious groups while secular liberalism is a united force over the whole world.

It's well above my paygrade to address this problem worldwide, but we can apply the lesson here. A coalition of social conservatives from any and every religious or non-religious hue must be built to exert maximum influence. Regardless of the "diversity is strength" mantra, it's a simple matter of arithmetic.

This diversity will mean that a special effort will be required to cooperate harmoniously, uniting on common moral ground instead of tangling over spiritual doctrine. That might sound like the classic dilution fallacy - if we can just avoid the controversial beliefs, we can all live in unity and the church will grow - but it is not. Evangelise away. Criticise other religious beliefs at will. Debate and defend. Just don't do it in the planning meeting for the joint campaign against assisted suicide.

We need to learn when presenting our values in explicitly Christian terms strengthens our case, and when it just alienates allies.

Whatever your theology of other religions, you must surely recognise a core of shared moral truth in each, reflecting our God given conscience. Uniting on issues of moral truth is perfectly compatible with disagreement over The Truth.

OVER TO YOU...

As a Christian, you have something powerful to bring into politics. Whether it's simply casting a wise vote, right up to elected office, you have benefited from God's revelation. When it comes to creating the best society for all, God knows best. The practicalities are open to debate, but the principles are secure. A dose of Christian truth can enable you to see through the bad ideas and good intentions of political parties and politicians. You can see what's really precious and where ultimate value lies.

Rejecting God's ways leads to tensions, degeneration and pain. As this becomes ever more apparent, we can offer truth that chimes with God-given consciences. A better way. Let the truth ring out for all to hear!

We are a minority, so we're not going to hold sway in our democratic system any time soon, but we can make a difference now and persuade ever more that our vision is worthy of consideration, then acceptance, then support, then implementation! To shift political debate, we need to be in it.

If we care about people - families, adults, children, the elderly – we'll care about politics.

My prayer is that you will fulfil your calling, support others in their calling, be brave, be wise and be effective.

If you are called to more direct involvement in politics, relish the opportunity! Many say that politics is "a dirty business". Maybe it is. But there's nothing dirty about bringing in truth, light, wisdom and integrity. And when Christian nay-sayers beset you with the debilitating lines that I've countered in these pages, this little book might help you to respond.

Richard Lucas

Leader of the Scottish Family Party

richard.lucas@scottishfamily.org